The Majesty of the
FRENCH QUARTER

Photography and Text by
Kerri McCaffety

Foreword by Mikko Macchione

PELICAN PUBLISHING COMPANY

Gretna 2000

The word "Pelican" and the depiction of a pelican are trademarks of Pelican Publishing Company, Inc., and are registered in the U.S. Patent and Trademark Office.

First printing, January 2000
Second printing, August 2000

Library of Congress Cataloging-in-Publication Data

McCaffety, Kerri
    The majesty of the French Quarter / text and photography by Kerri McCaffety ; foreword by Mikko Macchione.
        p.   cm.
        Includes bibliographical references.
        ISBN 1-56554-414-5 (hardcover : alk. paper)
        1. Architecture—Louisiana—New Orleans.   2. Interior decoration—Louisiana—New Orleans.   3. New Orleans (Louisiana)—Buildings, structures, etc.   4. Vieux Carré (New Orleans, La.)—Buildings, structures, etc.   I. Title.
    NA735.N4M35   1999
    976.3'35--dc21   99-40865
                                                                              CIP

Photo on front cover: *An 1820s Creole townhouse epitomizes eclectic Vieux Carré style with French antiques, musical instruments, voodoo dolls, and Carnival masks. Above the mantel is a painting commissioned by Napoleon's court celebrating the triumph of freedom in France (Lucy Burnett's home).*
Photo on back cover: *The garden of the Marchand Mansion.*
Photo on p. 2: *The fountain of the Hotel Maison DeVille on a cold morning. This hotel was once the home of Antoine Amadee Peychaud, inventor of the cocktail. Another of its famous residents was Tennessee Williams. The main house dates to 1800, and the older outbuildings survived the great fires.*
Photos on p. 7: *(left to right from top) Louisiana palms. Mardi Gras jester. Horse head hitching post. The courtyard of* Le Petit Théatre. *Xs made for luck on Marie Laveau's tomb. Balconies on Rampart Street. Sherry Haydel's bedroom. Rue Royale.*
Photo on p. 6: *The 1811 Campenel cottage.*
Photo on p. 8: *Grotto of Our Lady of Guadeloupe Chapel.*
Photo on p. 14: *Peter Patout's courtyard.*
Photo on p. 15: *Jon Vaccari's dining room.*

From *The View Carré—A General Statement* by Bernard Lemann, © 1996, used by permission of the author, Bernard Lemann.

Printed in Hong Kong

Published by Pelican Publishing Company, Inc.
1000 Burmaster Street, Gretna, Louisiana 70053

To the memory of my father, who made me want to do great things, and to the world's most wonderful women—my mother, Cynthia Reece McCaffety, and my sister, Lisa.

CONTENTS

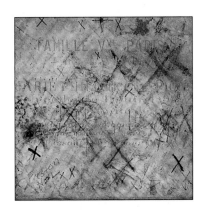

ACKNOWLEDGMENTS

People are the true majesty of the French Quarter—today's Vieux Carré residents add their unique touches to its on-going alchemy. These rooms are exquisitely beautiful because they reflect the spirit of the most fascinating and unorthodox group of people anywhere in the world. I was humbled by the eager generosity of new friends who took my hand and led me through the city I only thought I knew, especially Betty Norris, Betty Decell, and Ruth Bodenheimer.

Thank you to the people who let me into their homes and made me feel welcome: Rosemary James and Joe DeSalvo, Peter Yokum, Peter Patout, Julia Reed, Julie Smith, Jana Napoli, Missy Hodapp, Cher Boisfontaine Tharp, Lucy Burnett, Gregory Holt, Barbara Louviere, Jon Vaccari, Josephine Sacabo, Sherry Haydel, Emily Adams, Eugenie Schwartz, Susan Hoffman, Marilyn Young, Patrick Dunne, Ron Julian and Chuck Robinson, Nina Tyler, Buddy Arnold, Gordon Maginnis, Robert Sonnier, Pat and Lee Mason, and others.

I am grateful to the Quarter's dedicated advocates at the Historic New Orleans Collection, the Hermann-Grima and Gallier Houses, and the Beauregard-Keyes House.

New Orleans owes a great deal to the Vieux Carré Commission, whose work will afford future generations the gift of the French Quarter's beauty and romance.

I also owe much thanks to Mara Cooper for her delightful energy; Peter Woloszynski, my photography mentor, for the Hasselblad and the great stories; officer Jim O'Hern, who sees a different side of the French Quarter, for help and company; Hubie Vigreux, the spirit of New Orleans personified, who was my first guide to the city; and architect Malcolm Heard for writing the fabulous *French Quarter Manual*.

For various acts of generosity and kindness, love and thanks to Andrei Codrescu, Lee Meehan, Ellen Johnson, Merritt Doggins, Millie Ball, Marda Burton, Gavin Gassen, Winter C. Randall, and Gil Buras, and the people who shared their valuable ideas and expertise—Georgina Callan, Frank Masson, Allain Bush, Tom Delcambre, Debi Eagan, Darrell Chase, Jay Weigel, and "the Baroness" Shelley Poncy.

And I couldn't have written a paragraph without the genius Mikko Macchione.

FOREWORD
Hurricanes Know What it Means

Georges crept his way up the river. He'd annihilated Cuba and the Dominican Republic. Though the TV news drones chose to camp out in suburban high schools along with the suburban United Way to dramatically report the fears of the suburbanites, they did intersperse their commentary with announcements of temporary shelters in the Superdome and the Convention Center. Since New Orleans has had a grapevine, and diligent gossipmongers maintaining it, longer than most cities have had newspapers, those of us who live downtown got the scoop in a primeval way— word of mouth. We intently listened to the elders of the town who recalled the bygone storms as if mulling over long-departed school buddies—Juan, Betsy, Camille . . . some even recounted the Crevasse of '28. Grim recollections of water lapping the windowsills on top floors of the three-story French Quarter buildings circulated through the streets as if the water were already here and the storm a forgone memory.

"New Orleans you see," the anguished neo-local was quick to explain, "is like a tea cup poised below sea level between the river and the lake who are at sea level . . . " And that's just it, it was the neo-local, the recently (that is, since the last major flood) arrived who percolated stress and worry. They funereally iterated how the lower river is like a chute for hurricanes to come up. That this has never happened in the history of weather-keeping only seemed to confirm their mania—like doomsday to a zealot. The fact it hasn't happened only increases the importance of repentance 'cause it'll be here any day now!

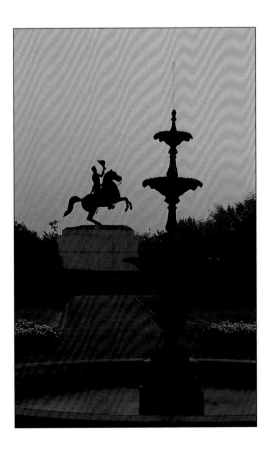

The point is this: almost everybody bailed out, and left the Quarter empty.

The French Quarter feels like a woman. Right behind the slender and upright St. Louis Cathedral is a sassy, but cuddly, vintage dress shoppe, Fleur de Paris, that hordes the very dresses that may have adorned Sarah Bernhardt and Jenny Lind. When the town was fresh and young she was seductive, voluptuous, and vulnerable—every ingredient essential in the composition of a great mistress. The finest clientele courted her and infused her with artistry, grace, style, and substance. There is so much expensive bric-a-brac in an antique shop window at the corner of Royal and Bienville Streets that the eye quickly discounts the lot; though any one piece would command the center of any table in Milwaukee. It is that last gift, substance, which her children are so quick to forget she possesses. Now, as the Live News8 Cam beams the perpetual fear from out in the malls, the faithless children look upon her aging beauty—alluring, but not as salable as she once was—and escape her bosom.

Usually Sunday mornings bring the line of visitors to Brennan's for "The Brunch." Wearing a fuchsia coat that would be called garish in Tulsa, Brennan's suffers the tromping in of the hungry and curious. Many aren't sure why they are there, only that it is expected of them to report back to their prosaic hamlets on the experience. "I'm just getting a salad," some proclaim. "I had all that New Orleans stuff last night." Gamely embracing their horrors, some of these outsiders actually break down and try the bread pudding. From breakdown to breakthrough—Brennan's, in the manner of the French Quarter, has charmed an unsuspecting voyeur into an enlightened inamorata.

Luckily for those of us who chose to hang for the storm, there weren't any lines of folks sticking around—most hit the road for Birmingham. I know one woman, freshly jilted, who rode in the same car with her ex-boyfriend, his new girlfriend, and HER two dogs and four cats. All of them,

down to the youngest kitten, are from Ohio. "Why Birmingham?" I asked. "Because of hotel space," I was told, as if I were the ingenuous one. I still don't know what that means. And I still can't understand why, to escape a storm, one would drive through it to get out and then drive back through it when it took the inevitable hard right they all take to slam the Gulf Coast of Mississippi and miss New Orleans altogether . . .

And what if I were washed into the Gulf by a deluge that scoured the Mississippi Delta, redirected the river into the Atchafalaya Basin, uprooted my mistress, and wiped away 300 years of quasi-European, extra-American culture? Would living in Birmingham be a better alternative?

The streets are empty. Decatur Street runs long and quiet by Café du Monde—the hectic center now strapped down under taut green tarps, past the statue of Andrew Jackson still brazenly rearing his horse as if ready to sail on the rising winds to his next adventure, all the way down to the normally raucous House of Blues—tonight slammed shut behind a cemetery gate. St. Philip Street lay as wide and empty as a St. Petersburg street after eleven, where the Russian police raise the bridges to discourage all-night carousing. A warm, steady, heady mist stings its way across the Quarter almost parallel to the ground. They closed up the floodgates behind the French Market over by Gallatin Street, an infamous stretch where prostitutes would help to shanghai visitors a hundred years ago. Today Jimmy Buffett and some fruit purveyors have business concerns there, and the worst experience for a tourist would be a traffic ticket, as the entire two blocks of this once-awesome street is unavailable for parking. There are to be no tickets that night—no cars. The mayor, a handsome, concerned-looking Creole, comes on the news to blossom on the grapevine. He imposes a curfew, and after that a solitary cop car zooms by less frequently than a streetcar. Not everything is closed, however.

All markets and employments are down. The restaurants are locked up. Only Kaldi's, the gutter-punk coffeehouse living in a stately former bank,

The Williams Residence at the Historic New Orleans Collection.

stays afloat. On one wall is a thirty-foot full-color sculpture of some ruddy-faced Bacchus tangling the vines of a coffee plantation. Underneath the mischievous avatar, baby-skinned street dwellers covered with piercings pour more milk into their lattés and stare at the architectural flourishes in the café that, except for the paganistic mural, could easily house a courtroom or a post office. But the babies don't need justice or a stamp—mama knows what they need.

The gay bars, instead of boarding up, also stay open. Where else could their public go? That many have nowhere else to comfortably live means Georges will just be another climatic inconvenience—like the humidity during a parade. Why shut the bars when many were staying by their mother? They sure as hell weren't going to Alabama. I'm not gay, but I'm staying, and if this is the Last Supper, so be it. Besides, I need a beer. We form a posse to raid a locked-down yuppie bar for twenty pounds of hamburger and a case of buns.

"What if this is it?" we thought to ourselves. Everyone always mentions New Orleans as the final third of the Chicago Fire/San Francisco Earthquake triumvirate of disasters. Imagine having the whole French Quarter to despoliate? To engender a new society? To be part of the heroic new guard to pick up where Bienville, O'Reilly, Jackson, Pontalba, and Moon Landrieu left off? Interesting that the city solons chose two of the most modern and ugly structures in which to house the refugees. We chose the Vieux Carré for the same reasons the original settlers did—it's the highest ground and it's easy to maintain an interesting life here.

The next morning, with all the nervous-nelly neos hunkered down in some fiction called the Deep South, and all the below-sea-level-locals eating hot dogs at the Superdome, we rise to a warm, partly cloudy day. The wind tirelessly whistles through the high tension wires over the French Market, no cars—not even police—whiz by. Jackson Square's only occupant is the one for whom it was named. He still sits high on his horse in front of the placid cathedral and tests the breeze with his hat. Out on the river, by the Brewery, the abandoned Creole Queen dock snaps to a violent flapping. The tarp furls out over the water, barely clinging to its last two stakes in the ground, flicking as if a washerwoman were, laundry-like, spreading out a sheet. The "sheet" was formerly a massive tent under which hundreds of passengers could wait. No one around now to tie down the tarp. The Queen herself holds fast to the pier and gently absorbs the petulant river beneath her.

The French Quarter remains. The storm took that habitual right turn last night and is walloping a place no one cares about—not even those that live there. For thirty-six hours the woman that protected me, fed me, taught me to dance, and seduced me to sleep at her breast has been all mine. At noon, while CNN is still telling my far-flung friends and relations that New Orleans is in dire danger, the sun comes out, causing a brief rainbow downriver. The lady puts on her face. I didn't abandon her and she stayed.

by Mikko Macchione

*Yet beauty lingers here. To say nothing of the pic-
turesque, sometimes you get sight of comfort, sometimes of opulence, through the unlatched wicket in
some* porte-cochère—*red-painted brick pavement,
foliage of dark palm or pale banana, marble or
granite masonry and blooming parterres; . . .*

or through a chink between some pair of heavy batten window-shutters, opened with an almost reptile wariness, your eye gets a glimpse of lace and brocade upholstery, silver and bronze, and much similar rich antiquity.
—George W. Cable, Old Creole Days, *1879*

SYMPHONY IN A SWAMP
Prelude

Architecture in general is frozen music.
—Friedrich Von Schelling, 1809

If architecture is frozen music, the French Quarter plays a symphony of three centuries and a myriad of cultures. Its strange, harmonic beauty could only have come about in a European outpost on the edge of the Caribbean at the dawn of the United States.

In 1718 French convicts cleared less than a mile of wet ground at a curve in the Mississippi River—the beginning of a colony that would become America's most romantic city, set to the tempo of horse-drawn carriages, tap dancers, and the adagio of the River herself.

Locals call it the Vieux Carré (French for "old square"), and for a hundred years the small grid comprised the whole city of New Orleans, with plantations and swamps on its outskirts. The old square today forms a window to the city's past. From the first French settlers who struggled against the waterlogged land, storms, fires, and yellow fever; to the Spaniards who wove their melody into the song of a French city; to African slaves, free people of color, Irish, English, German, and Sicilian immigrants—they all left their legacy in its hundred square blocks.

A view of the Upper Pontalba through the arches of the Cabildo.

16

Named for the French Regent, the Duc d'Orleans, the colony began as the original real estate scam. In the seventeenth century, a powerful, greedy France played a game of chess with Spain and England, marching over the New World to exploit its natural resources of farmland, gold, and silver. In 1716, a Scottish gambler, John Law, tossed the dice that still roll today. Law convinced the Duke of Orleans to sell shares in a Louisiana settlement

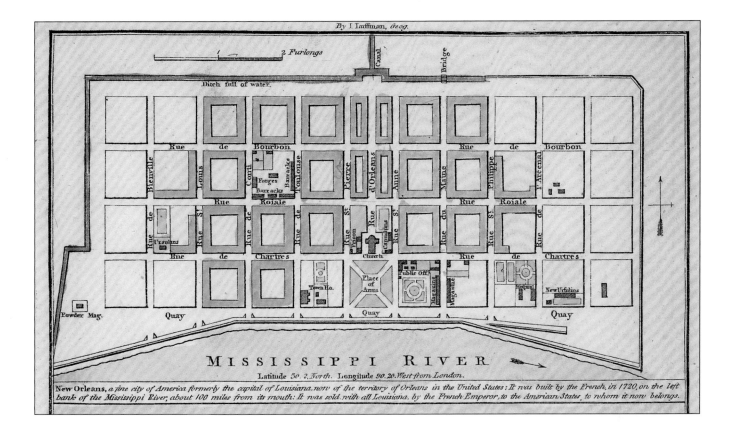

By I. Luffman, Geog.

New Orleans, a fine city of America, formerly the capital of Louisiana, now of the territory of Orleans in the United States: It was built by the French, in 1720, on the left bank of the Mississippi River, about 100 miles from its mouth: It was sold, with all Louisiana, by the French Emperor, to the American States, to whom it now belongs.

based on its potential wealth as a port connecting all of North America to the world. Few volunteers chose to leave France for the mosquito-ridden swampland, so prisons were emptied and peasants were kidnapped to populate the remote settlement. The city engineers, along with a third of the colonists, died of yellow fever. A flood wiped out the village in its first year. And as the colony floundered, Law sold increasingly worthless shares until, with the French monarchy deep in debt and the economic plan washed up, Law fled France.

While a thousand years of the French monarchy started its march to the guillotine, the colony it spawned survived. Eventually, the few rough blocks laid out in French military outpost style started to look like a city. The grid along the river that would become the French Quarter, as drawn by Le Blond de la Tour in 1721, included walled fortifications. Perhaps because the colony, referred to as "the island of Orleans," had swampland as a natural moat and was a financial disaster, the planned walls were never built. Mud ramparts stood roughly where the border streets of the Quarter exist today—Canal Street, Rampart Street, and Esplanade Avenue.

Crescendo

Those of French or Spanish parentage born in the New World were called "Creole," from the Spanish *criado,* meaning brought up or reared. United in their isolation and struggle for survival, Creoles, Africans, and a spectrum of immigrants created a new culture. These independent souls, caught between old and new worlds, rebuilt their city after fires and storms, and a hundred years after its founding, the Quarter map looked much as it does today. In the nineteenth century, New Orleans became the busiest port in the world and the wealthiest, most sophisticated and debauched city in America.

With Latin fervor and access to the riches of the world, New Orleans developed a taste for the finest of Paris, from absinthe to opera, and extravagant pleasures from cuisine to cocottes.

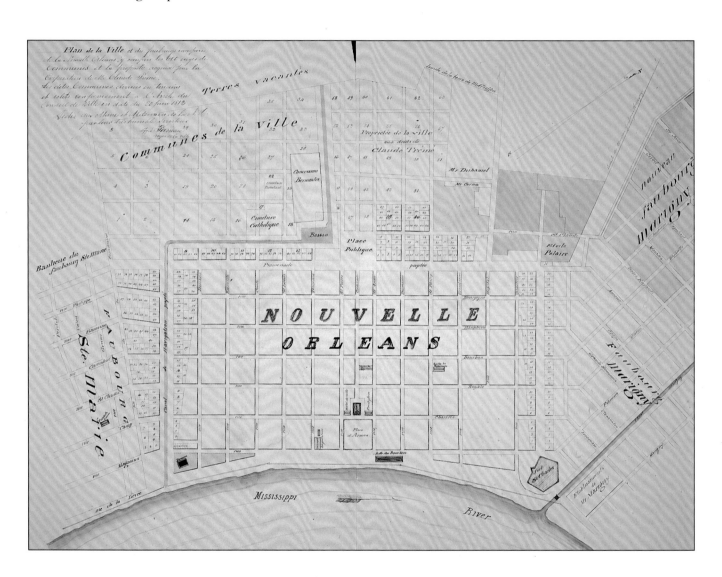

And what fun to eat all you wanted without having censorious people say you weren't lady-like. And what fun to drink all the champagne you pleased.

—Margaret Mitchell,
Scarlett O'Hara in Gone With The Wind, *1936*

Antoine's, the South's oldest restaurant, opened in 1840 and still serves French Creole dishes in an 1831 mansion.

The Gumbo Shop opened in 1945 and serves rich New Orleans fare in a 1795 Creole townhouse. Artist Marc Anthony painted the murals depicting an early nineteenth-century Jackson Square.

Tujague's opened across the street from the French Market in 1856 to serve the local workers when Levee Street (now Decatur Street) was the center of New Orleans' commerce. The 1827 building occupies the site of an old Spanish armory.

19

New Orleans' intimate interplay of cultures would give birth to jazz in the red-light district of Storyville, just outside the French Quarter, around 1900.

Jazz Café.

Bourbon Street started swinging to the beat of burlesque and glorified vice right after World War II. But among the strip clubs, souvenir shops, and daiquiri bars, fine homes and cafés of a grand era endure.

Charles Etienne Gayarré, one of the first historians of Louisiana, lived at 601 Bourbon Street.

The Bourbon Street mansion of Lindy Boggs, former Congresswoman and current Ambassador to the Vatican.

Built in 1831, this Bourbon Street townhouse has been the address of America's finest French bistro, Galatoire's, since 1905.

Behind the mad façade of Bourbon Street are
quiet rooms filled with fine antiques.

Creole flowers drape over a Federal banquet table in a home on Bourbon Street.

Third Empire candelabras stand against engravings of the expulsion of the popes from Avignon in this 1830s Bourbon Street apartment.

Built in 1806, Jack Sutton's antique gallery housed the well-known pharmacy of François Grandchamps in the early 1800s.

Rue Royal has been a fashionable commercial avenue since the early 1800s. Collectors from around the world come to New Orleans to savor Royal Street's antique shops and galleries.

Patout Antiques seduces passersby from the Kohn buildings, built in 1840.

Rothchild's Antiques has been on Royal Street since 1933.

General Jean Labatut, appointed by Andrew Jackson to defend the city during the Battle of New Orleans, built a one-story house, now Harris Antiques, in approximately 1785.

Labatut hired important local architects Pinson and Pizetta to add a second floor in 1821. The third floor dates to the nineteenth century.

The pre-eminence of the Quarter's boutiques, filled with Old World treasures and antebellum heirlooms, is rivaled only by the splendor of its hidden rooms and gardens. Often above a store—as they were two hundred years ago—the apartments along Royal are elegant *mise-en-scènes* for the drama of French Quarter life.

Fleur de Paris occupies the first floor of this 1827 building, and above the store, on the second floor, is the salon of Rosemary James' Faulkner House Designs (right).

The 1857 Gallier House in summer dress.

The double parlor of the 1838 Miltenberger House.

A fountain at the 1794 Montegut House.

THE HEARTBEAT OF THE VIEUX CARRÉ

The Place d'Armes, originally a military parade ground, was renamed Jackson Square in 1851. The square has hosted the colony's official events for generations and today is a public garden, providing a backdrop for painters, jazz bands, and fortunetellers. The bronze statue of General Andrew Jackson on horseback rears before St. Louis Cathedral—a sight that signifies New Orleans the way the Eiffel Tower stands for Paris or the Alamo for San Antonio.

The town's center memorializes a pivotal event in American history and its unlikely hero. Trade disputes with England had escalated into a bitter impasse that became the War of 1812. After two years of battles, British troops burned Washington D.C. in 1814 and then headed for the financial lifeblood of the Union, its most important port, New Orleans. "The island" cared little about what happened in the rest of America. The Creoles in the

The Battle of New Orleans is depicted in a mosaic at the Ursuline Convent, where nuns kept an all-night vigil, praying for victory. A commemorative mass is said at the convent every year on the anniversary of the battle.

city hated the idea of being a part of the United States and resented the ill-mannered Americans moving in. The cultural melting pot was at a boil. New Orleans' divergent coteries clashed so badly that eventually the city would be divided into separate municipalities. After the bloody uprising in St. Dominique, whites feared their slaves. Indians posed a shadowy threat on the outskirts. The American governor, Claiborne, plotted against the city's favorite procurer of black market luxuries and illegal slaves, Jean Lafitte. Into this apoplectic apathy rode a gaunt stranger, Andrew Jackson.

Although suffering from malaria, Jackson decisively readied New Orleans to defend itself. He declared martial law in response to the British threat and recruited every willing man for the impending battle. The bars of the French Quarter, normally full of sailors and laborers, were empty, and the city's businesses and government offices closed. Jackson rallied a rainbow of Creoles, Spanish, free men of color, and Choctaw Indians. Ignoring the governor, Jackson arranged pardons for Lafitte and his men in exchange for the pirate's stockpile of guns and ammunition. Together with riflemen from Tennessee and Kentucky, the general's army totaled about four thousand men. They would face an army of ten thousand seasoned British soldiers.

On the foggy morning of January 8, 1815, Jackson's troops intercepted the British advance at a plantation six miles down river from the French Quarter. Both sides were unaware that a peace treaty officially ending the War of 1812 had been signed two weeks before. The odd array of Creoles, riflemen, Indians, and pirates fired from behind a mud rampart as the British crossed the open field, and in less than two hours, two thousand British soldiers, including three generals, were dead.

The Battle of New Orleans was the last of four strategic twists that kept the city out of the reach of England. Before the colony was even founded, Bienville's ship, while searching for a suitable spot to found a settlement, met a British ship doing the same. The French captain lied to the English, telling them a French colony had already been established. The duped British captain gave up and turned his ship around at a place in the river now called English Turn. Then, in 1763, the Seven Years War forced the transfer of much of France's holdings in America to England. But rather than give up New Orleans, Louis XV secretly gave it to his cousin, King Charles III of Spain. Forty years later, shortly after Napoleon had regained the colony for France, French armies were again embroiled in a war with England, and Napoleon's troops were losing a battle against the slave rebels in Haiti. Bonaparte felt he could not defend New Orleans, and he sold the Louisiana Territory to the new United States, again, so the British wouldn't get it. Finally, the U.S. and Andrew Jackson protected New Orleans from the British attack in 1815. And so, the Union Jack never flew over the Vieux Carré.

Fearing for their lives, the women of New Orleans waited for their husbands to return from the Chalmette Battlefield in 1815. From this balcony they heard the cries of victory. Madame Poreé's, built before 1808.

A hundred or more ladies—"the flowers of society"—gathered at the residence of Madame Poreé—a house which is still standing at the corner of Royal and Dumaine streets and spent the night prior to January 8th. . . . They huddled together in the large parlors, behind the tight-barred windows. Candles were burning, and the women knelt, praying the long hours through.

Lyle Saxon, Lafitte the Pirate, *1930*

THE ARCHITECTURAL OPUS OF JACKSON SQUARE

In the entire Louisiana Purchase territory, a chunk roughly one third of the United States, no great architecture existed until Gilbert Guillemard designed the St. Louis Cathedral, the Cabildo, and the Presbytère on the French Quarter's Place d'Armes. The current St. Louis Cathedral was rebuilt in 1852 by the prominent French architect J.N.B. dePouilly and reflects the Greek Revival style of the time.

St. Louis Cathedral bears the name of the patron saint of Bourbon, France. The first church on the site was destroyed by the hurricane of 1722, and prayers are still offered to Our Lady of Prompt Succor to save the city from destruction every hurricane season.

Named for the local Spanish governing body, the Cabildo is the most important building of the Spanish Colonial era. Completed in 1803, it incorporates bits of an earlier 1750s building. In the year of its completion, the Cabildo would see the Spanish, French, and American flags fly over the Place d'Armes. In the Cabildo jail, Jean Lafitte's brother and partner in crime, Pierre, was held in chains from April to September 1814 before escaping shortly before the Battle of New Orleans.

The Cabildo and its twin, the Presbytère, completed in 1813, now house exhibits of the Louisiana State Museum.

The front arches of the Cabildo.

The front hall of the Cabildo and the flags that flew over the city.

In the Cabildo's Sala Capitular, the transfer of the colony resulting from the Louisiana Purchase was made official.

The Pontalba Building.

The initials for Almonester and Pontalba intertwine in the cast iron balconies.

Jackson Square was a family affair. The Baroness de Pontalba, Micaela Almonester, worked with architects James Gallier, Sr., and Henry Howard to design Parisian-style apartments flanking Jackson Square. Her father, Andres Almonester de Roxas, funded the cathedral and the Cabildo half a century earlier.

Jackson Square, and all of the French Quarter around it, opens up on the Mississippi River, the third largest river in the world.

St. Louis Cathedral from the river.

The steamboat Creole Queen *and the Crescent City Connection.*

Along the river at the edge of Jackson Square, the French Market occupies a trading site established by Indians at the founding of the colony.

Café du Monde serves coffee and beignets in the oldest surviving French Market structure, built in 1813 by the eminent architect-builders Claude Gurlie and Joseph Guillot.

Nearing its tricentennial, the French Quarter retains its original city plan, its Latin *joie de vivre,* and the religion of its founders—Roman Catholic tradition soaks the air like humidity in the French Quarter. New Orleans is a corner of America where rosary beads hang on a *priedieu.*

Candles burn for remembered souls at Our Lady of Guadeloupe Chapel, 1826, New Orleans' oldest surviving church. Irene's Restaurant (right) pours out Sicilian gratitude in the form of wine, braided bread, and pasta on St. Joseph's Day.

New Orleans may be genuflecting at the altar of Roman Catholicism, eating fish on Fridays, and hailing Mary on Sunday mornings, but *nobody* sins like a Catholic.

Centuries ago, the Roman Catholic Church adopted an ancient, pagan spring fertility ritual that it could not suppress. In the nineteenth century, the French Quarter, a Catholic culture with a pagan heart, lustfully embraced the pre-Lenten bacchanal, and every year Mardi Gras gushes into the French Quarter with a river of liquor and merriment.

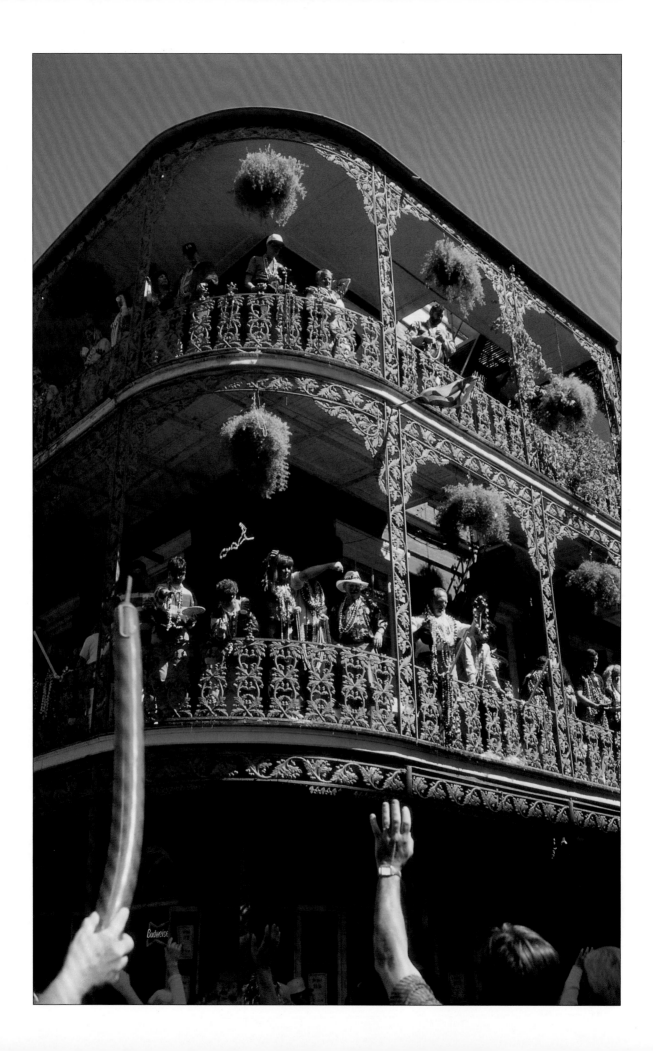

On Fat Tuesday in the French Quarter, masked revelers swarm under balconies over-filled with rowdy onlookers.

In the powerful spell of New Orleans, time slows, the outside world vanishes, and an unplanned and ever-changing gallery of shapes and colors grows from the ground, crumbles from the walls, or stretches with the setting sun.

The garden of Lucullus Antiques.

The 1811 Campenel cottage.

The weathered front of Preservation Hall, an 1817 townhouse and world-famous traditional jazz venue.

The wealth of the world is here—unworked gold in the ore. The paradise of the South is here, deserted and half in ruins. I never beheld anything so beautiful and so sad.

—*Lafcadio Hearn,*
Lafcadio Hearn, Life and Letters, *1877*

This stoic house on Chartres Street opens onto a French Quarter Eden in back.

THE CITY'S HIDDEN MELODY

. . . of all secret cities, New Orleans, so it seems to me, is the most secretive, the most unlike, in reality, what an outsider is permitted to observe. The prevalence of steep walls, of obscuring foliage, of tall thick locked iron gates, of shuttered windows, of dark tunnels leading to overgrown gardens where mimosa and camellias contrast colors, and lazing lizards, flicking their forked tongues, race along palm fronds—all this is not accidental decor, but architecture deliberately concocted to camouflage, to mask, as at a Mardi Gras Ball, the lives of those born to live among these protective edifices.
—*Truman Capote,* Hidden Gardens, *1975*

The first residents of the city, in urban-European style, built houses right at the sidewalk, or banquette, and walled the spaces between. The French Quarter's blocks, still closed from the outside, form an outer wall giving protection from intruders and hurricanes, and hiding the secret majesty within. The beauty of Vieux Carré homes is focused at the rear, in contrast to the grand front entrances and lawns of St. Charles Avenue.

It would be impossible to guess from Barracks Street that this cottage has one of the prettiest courtyards in the Vieux Carré.

A Dauphine Street cottage hides a courtyard and pool behind.

915 St. Ann Street.

While front windows are often rectangular and shuttered, back windows of the same house fan sunlight into an exquisite variety of arches.

Dr. Deveze's House on Royal Street, 1830.

The Jacob House on Toulouse Street, 1813.

The Montegut House, 1794.

Old New Orleans, for all its lavish lifestyle, wore a very humble disguise until American influence crept in during the nineteenth century. Greek Revival and Philadelphia red brick came into vogue by the mid-1800s. Before hard bricks were imported, the sandy local bricks had to be covered with wood or stucco. Exposed brick looked unfinished and became unfashionable in old Creole days.

The Hermann-Grima House, 1831.

The Victor David House, 1838.

One of the finest examples of Greek Revival architecture in the United States is the Marble Hall of the U.S. Custom House on Canal Street, 1848-1881. Fourteen Corinthian columns tower fifty-four feet high.

Greek Revival, fluted Ionic column on Esplanade Avenue, 1839.

The back of St. Louis Cathedral, 1852. French architect J.N.B. de Pouilly's version of Greek Revival.

51

The Pontalba buildings (on the right), inspired by Paris apartments, show Greek Revival influence with American red brick but maintain the Creole inner courtyard and commercial/residential tradition, while the buildings across Chartres Street (on the left) retain the stuccoed fronts of an older Creole taste.

Balconies and Courtyards: The Spanish Serenade

The first revolution in North America took place when New Orleans' three thousand French citizens found out that their colony had been given to Spain. In 1768 a group of the city's prominent men threw out the first Spanish governor, Ulloa, in a bloodless revolution. Those in New Orleans with powerful and lucrative positions wanted things to stay exactly as they were. King Charles III responded by sending Count Alexander O'Reilly, an Irish general in the Spanish army. O'Reilly and his two thousand six hundred troops took New Orleans by force and executed the leaders of the revolt.

But even as Spanish rule took hold, things did stay much as they were. The two countries shared a common religion. The Spanish officials spoke French, married French women, reported conscientiously to their superiors in Havana, and interfered very little with the economy of corrupt Nouvelle Orleans.

French lifestyles and building styles dominated throughout Spanish rule and continued years after the Louisiana Purchase. A new tidal wave of French traditions hit New Orleans at the beginning of the nineteenth century thanks in part to a brutal slave uprising in the West Indies.

The colony called St. Dominique, now Haiti, had produced enormous wealth for the French crown, exporting cotton, sugar, coffee, and indigo to the continent. Slaves eventually outnumbered whites more than four to one and revolted in the 1790s, massacring most of the white plantation owners and their families.

From 1792 to 1812, over ten thousand St. Dominique refugees, French Creoles, poured into New Orleans, doubling the city's population. Along with a fresh infusion of French heritage, they brought with them a mixture of Catholicism and West African religion called voodoo.

With Spain no longer in charge after 1803, many Spaniards left for Cuba, while in Europe, the French Revolution sent its own refugees, the so-called "foreign French," to New Orleans.

The open but covered area, or loggia, of Lucy Burnett's Creole townhouse.

Today's Vieux Carré reflects French building practices of the seventeenth century with an openness that evolved as the architecture responded to the rainy and hot environment.

The forty years of Spanish possession blew through the colony like a sultry breeze and left as its signature the most romantic of spaces—exquisite balconies and glorious courtyards.

Throughout Spanish Colonial times, wrought iron railed balconies were imported from Spain and Mexico or forged in New Orleans.

The dainty wrought iron railings of the Chesneau House, circa 1800.

The Casa Correjolles shows the finest example of early wrought iron craftsmanship.

In the 1850s, the Pontalba buildings changed the face of New Orleans with their bold new cast iron galleries. These verandas could be quite large because of their column-supports, unlike the wood or wrought iron balconies before them that were supported by the building.

Huge ornamental cast iron galleries were added to many existing buildings in the 1850s, extending living space out over the sidewalks.

900 Royal went up in 1838 and the "lace iron" galleries were added in 1858.

The Labranche Building at 700 Royal Street was built in 1840, but the galleries were added many years later.

The 1840 Kohn Building, 920 Royal Street, received its galleries in the 1850s.

At the corner of Dauphine Street and Ursuline Street, the Gardette-LePretre House went up in 1836 but was without galleries until the 1850s.

Examples of all kinds of balconies and galleries hang daintily from buildings or stand audaciously over the street today, providing a premium French Quarter view.

The inner courtyard of the Languille House has wood railings.

800 Royal Street. When Francisco Balthazar Languille built this house in 1801, it was the highest building in the city. It was topped a few years later by the Pedesclaux-LeMonnier House.

The same house has a wrought iron upper balcony and a cast iron lower balcony facing the street.

Don Bartolome Bosque's house exemplifies Spanish colonial architecture from 1795. The sprawling house surrounds a grand courtyard entered through the carriageway, or *porte-cochère*. Bosque, a Spaniard, and his French wife had a daughter, Suzette, a renowned beauty who became the third wife of the American governor, W.C.C. Claiborne. After his death, she married John Randolph Grimes, the lawyer of the pirates Lafitte. The Bosque House occupies the site where the first great fire started in 1788.

While activity along French Quarter streets at times borders on the chaotic, the back garden remains a quiet paradise.

Behind a house on Royal Street, beyond the servant's quarters, lies a hidden garden known as Daniel Clark's patio. Irishman Daniel Clark served as the American consul to Spanish colonial Louisiana in the 1790s and lived here in 1803. A brilliant businessman and politician, Clark was infamous for his connection to Jean Lafitte and his animosity for the American governor, Claiborne, whom he shot in the leg in a duel in 1806.

Clark is said to have given President Jefferson the idea to buy Louisiana. He died a bachelor in 1813, spawning the longest, most sensational legal battle of the nineteenth century. His illegitimate daughter, Myra Clark Gaines, spent most of her life fighting for her inheritance.

The courtyard pool of the Hotel Ste. Helene.

Tennessee Williams enjoyed this blooming hideaway behind his Dumaine Street apartment.

The Montegut garden.

A fantastic fountain in the courtyard of the Girod House, now the New Orleans Pharmacy Museum.

REQUIEM

Grand tombs adorned with imported marble and fresh flowers stand beside collapsing ruins of bare brick and stucco. The architecture of St. Louis Cemetery echoes the French Quarter on a smaller scale. St. Louis Cemetery No. 1 opened on the edge of the French Quarter in 1788, and it was here that above-ground crypts first appeared. Before 1788 the dead were buried on the riverbank or in a graveyard that existed near St. Peter and Burgundy. The tombs of St. Louis Cemetery No. 1 are footprints of history, a chronicle of the region's wars, plagues, economy, and spirituality.

The colonial powers that shaped the French Quarter lent their traditions to its burial grounds. The wall vaults that enclose the cemetery, called ovens or *fours* in French, were used in Spain's colonies all over the New World. The society or group crypts, often the largest and most elaborately

On a society tomb in St. Louis Cemetery, a sculpture succumbs to the elements.

decorated structures, are also a legacy from Spanish rule. As with French Quarter building practices, while some Spanish traditions took hold, the majority of burials in St. Louis Cemetery No. 1 were in the French style—single-family crypts.

The oldest of these tombs are simple rectangular brick structures, plastered and whitewashed, large enough for two chambers for caskets, one above the other, and a crypt below for bones. After a given time the caskets could be removed and burned, and the bones deposited in the crypt. In this way, the tomb served a family for generations. The names of the deceased are written on a slab of imported marble covering the front of the tomb.

During Colonial years New Orleans cemeteries were overfilled by repeated epidemics. Brick entombment became law during the yellow fever epidemics in the early 1800s, when the belief was that the illness came from the stench from the cemeteries. St. Louis Cemetery No. 1 was filled by 1820. New cemeteries were placed outside the city, which was just beginning to spread beyond the French Quarter.

Along with other important architects, J. N. B. dePouilly, who designed alterations to the St. Louis Cathedral, contributed to the cemeteries. In Paris, dePouilly had made sketches of the Greek Revival tombs in Père Lachaise Cemetery that he brought to New Orleans as models for his tomb designs.

The very craftsmen who forged the lovely balconies in the French Quarter added their art to the cities of the dead in the nineteenth century as well. Some tombs are surrounded by ornate wrought iron fences with gates.

Family crypts.

A CHORUS OF ARCHITECTURAL LEGACIES

Early eighteenth-century traditions molded the French Quarter we see today, but very few structures survive from the first fifty years of life in the colony. Floods, fires, hurricanes, and time ruined most of the constructions. More than a thousand French Quarter buildings were reduced to

embers by huge fires in 1788 and 1794. Practically the entire city was rebuilt by its ten thousand inhabitants at the end of the eighteenth century.

The only intact building of the French colonial period housed the Ursuline nuns, who came to the New World in 1727 to educate young girls and nurse the sick. The Ursuline Convent, at 1114 Chartres, was completed in 1752. Its provincial Louis XV, or Baroque, style—also the style of the first St. Louis Cathedral—typifies French architecture of the early-eighteenth century.

Ursuline Convent, 1752.

The cypress staircase is the oldest piece of architecture in the Mississippi Valley. It survives from the earlier 1727 convent and was altered to fit the existing building.

632 Dumaine typifies French Colonial architecture of New Orleans' early days. This plantation-style house, with a raised basement and steep roof, emerged in subtropical climates. Every room opens onto wide verandas in front and back. This type of veranda had canvas flaps that could be rolled down to close the area completely in bad weather or hot sun.

The house became known as Madame John's Legacy after George Washington Cable used it as the home of a fictional character in his short story, "'Tite Poulette." Cable's writing introduced a large audience to the exotic city of New Orleans in the late nineteenth century, and many buildings are remembered more for their fictional inhabitants than for the real ones.

The first house on the site, built in the 1730s, burned in the 1788 fire. But Don Manuel de Lanzos, a Spanish officer, had builders use the original home as a model for the 1788 construction. Rene Beluche, lieutenant of Jean Lafitte's pirate band, lived here in the early nineteenth century.

Madame John's Legacy, (top) now a part of the Louisiana State Museum. Front gallery of Madame John's Legacy (bottom).

A framed work of art—the winding stairway of the 1808 Marchand Mansion.

A leaning loggia window is a part of the strange jigsaw puzzle that is the Pedesclaux-LeMonnier House, designed c. 1794.

On the site of the old U. S. barracks on Governor Nichols Street, this 1846 house makes the most of an odd little lot. It is two stories high, one room deep and one room wide (22' x 16'). A window has been set into a door opening.

House Types

Houses in the Vieux Carré fall roughly into five categories: the Creole cottage, the Spanish Colonial house, the townhouse, the shotgun house, and various service structures. But the buildings refuse to follow strict chronological order. Linear time, like a drunken tourist, gets lost and wanders happily up and down the streets of the Vieux Carré. Types and styles of architecture overlap, revert, and combine. New pieces adorn old buildings. Old pieces and traditions show up in new buildings. A few houses salute the street and announce their type, and some structures wink and offer a clue. Sometimes the houses are as irregular and crooked as the town's story.

In the modern French Quarter renaissance, there is a new admiration for the artful forms of architectural features whose functionality has long passed. These homes were built a hundred years before cars and air-conditioning with *porte-cochères* designed for horse-drawn carriages and windows and transoms their only source of ventilation. Careful renovations bring into the twenty-first century rooms that were designed before electricity and plumbing. Those who love the Vieux Carré's romantic past have removed the dropped ceilings of recent years and restored buildings to their intended grandeur. Historians have scraped through the centuries to find original paint colors, so that French Quarter streets are again a parade of reds and yellows shuttered in Napoleon blue or Paris green.

Symmetry pleased the eye of old New Orleans. Rooms were square and equal in size without bathrooms or kitchens to intrude on their space. As a part of that visual flow, decorative armoires and chests were preferred over closets.

We should let the French Quarter style change our lives rather than destroy the beauty of its architecture adapting it to us. People lived happily in these houses for more than a hundred years. Why not have the kitchen in the slave quarters?

—*Frank W. Masson, AIA*

ANCIENT SONGS WITH AN ISLAND RYTHYM

The traditions of seventeenth-century Paris, influenced since the Renaissance by Italian, Moorish, Dutch, and German designs, flowed across the Atlantic and picked up bits of the British Isles, the Caribbean, and Africa. All were tossed into twentieth-century America and infused by the French Quarter's lust for creativity. Something powerful emerged.

All this French style, Spanish romance, mud, mosquitoes, and religion became today's French Quarter *je ne sais quoi*. Reminders of ancestry, voodoo, and Mardi Gras sit on the mantels and hang on the walls.

French Provincial elegance, urban-Louisiana style—Peter Patout's Bourbon Street home.

A new, Old-World luxury glows in the French Quarter residence of designer Sherry Haydel. The wall pattern was made with a stencil, a decorative tool that came to Europe from the East in medieval times. The bench is a new Haydel creation.

From period perfection to eclectic decay, French Quarter rooms can shine with bold color or embrace a sophisticated bohemian disrepair.

A portrait of Lucien Hermann hangs above an Empire sofa in the 1831 Hermann-Grima House.

Artist Josephine Sacabo's studio in the 1800 Chesneau House.

A twist in the personalities of New Orleanians makes for some fascinating interiors. The Vieux Carré's great rooms entertain the eye and stimulate the imagination with items of character and patinas earned with age. In objets d'art, as in people, the French Quarter prefers the slightly imperfect, the interestingly scarred.
—Allain Bush, antiques dealer

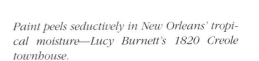

Paint peels seductively in New Orleans' tropical moisture—Lucy Burnett's 1820 Creole townhouse.

A Royal Street stairwell transverses 166 years of weather and ruin.

A turquoise and ochre palette emerged when the wallpaper was stripped from these walls in the 1834 Prevost House.

Freedom raps out the underlying rhythm of the city that care forgot. Never a place for conformity, the Vieux Carré encourages eccentricity, sometimes even exhibitionism. The same spirit that spawned jazz and shocked Protestants in the nineteenth century shows up in a glorious caravan of scarlet and gold, in unexpected pieces nailed to the wall or draped around the room like a scene from Salome.

Novelist Julie Smith felt free to emulate something that never existed in her Marrakech-meets-Storyville boudoir (left). A Haitian voodoo flag, musical instruments, and a Mardi Gras mask throw in a spice of New Orleans (top). Designer Betty Norris draped the room with shimmering fabrics and hung the windows with a rainbow of Indian saris. With decorative painter Susan Norris, Betty created the red-bordered gold wall finish (bottom).

"The Sun King," Louis XIV, would have been proud of this radiant extravagance.

Designer Emily Adam's spiritual/animal allegory in her Pontalba apartment.

The purple Empire of designer Rosemary James in the 1840 Faulkner House.

In New Orleans, spirituality and style are one and the same. Beauty, amusement, God, and Napoleon are treated with equal zeal as traditions and furniture pass from parents to children along with genes.

1850s portraits of Mrs. Alcée Villeré and Judah Philip Benjamin hang in the Victorian Gallery of the Merieult House, a part of the Historic New Orleans Collection, built in 1792.

There is an intellectual exuberance that permeates French Quarter interiors. They are expressions of New Orleans' rich European heritage, softened by several centuries of Southern exposure. Rooms are scaled for a lifestyle no longer lived and whisper of Rome, Barcelona or Paris. The extravagant volume of the interior spaces, in an increasingly crowded world, sparks a memory of something we have never known.
　　　　—Georgina O'Hara Callan, designer and
　　　　　　　author of The Encyclopedia of Fashion

The Kohn Building.

French Quarter interiors dazzle with the Easter egg colors of Versailles or flirt with earth tones and shades of white.

Missy Hodapp's bedroom, in an 1810 cottage, is an inspiration in white/Caribbean. The headboard is a nineteenth-century French fan window.

Gregory Holt's 1827 townhouse calms with the ivory refinement of antique silk and Fortuny chandeliers. A painting of Mardi Gras in Venice by Jurgen Gorg hangs above a Parisian settee.

The Creole Cottage

The Creole cottage brings medieval architecture into the twenty-first century here in the French Quarter, where it mixes it with Colonial, antebellum, and contemporary styles—sometimes all at once.

Its form gives us a view of the past. A relative of the medieval French Provincial half-timber house, the Creole cottage consists of four square rooms with no halls and a rear gallery. Two back-to-back fireplaces serve the four rooms. Most cottages are set at the sidewalk, with a two-story service structure at the back of the lot and a paved courtyard between.

The cottages in the French Quarter were built from the late 1700s to the mid-1800s. Originally the brick and posts construction, or *briquettè entre poteaux,* was covered with stucco or wood to protect it from moisture.

A Creole cottage on Dauphine Street (top left), built in 1825 for Louisa Baptiste Boux, a free woman of color. An 1830 Bourbon Street cottage (top right) has been returned to its original colors and has a rare pan tile roof. At 901 Burgundy Street (bottom left) sits one of the few houses in the French Quarter built before the two great fires. This house survived because it wasn't here. Some time prior to 1777, this cottage sat on Gabriel Peyroux's plantation on Bayou Road and was moved to this French Quarter site in 1781. A 1780s cottage (bottom right), now a part of the Chateau Hotel. The Audubon Cottage (right) was the home of wildlife painter John James Audubon and his family in 1821-22.

This 1820s Creole cottage has an 1850s Greek Revival façade but retains its original four-room layout inside. Arranged in traditional Creole style, the parlor and dining room are on one side and the bedrooms on the other. New Orleans designer Rodney Villarreal worked with the owner to combine antique family pieces with new in a way that enhances the yielding beauty of the house.

The enclosed back gallery forms a tropical transition from house to garden.

Artist Cher Boisfontaine Tharp's paintings add exotic colors to her 1816 Creole cottage and slave quarters. The cottage's four-square-room construction has been altered to create a long parlor on one side where sparse elegance surrounds Boisfontaine's painting titled *It's a Jungle in There.*

A purple ape presides over the first floor of the slave quarters in Boisfontaine's painting called *Gorilla Warfare*.

A back-to-back fireplace opens in the parlor and the bedroom of the Tharp's cottage, where ostrich eggs and an old map of New Orleans form a study in shades of white.

The service building hides a secret garden, seen through a window with original ramshorn hinges.

One of the French Quarter's most beautiful stairways ascends the back gallery of Gordon Hobson Maginnis' cottage. The grand house was built in 1815 for the Cazelar family, free people of color. Two kitchens facing the courtyard replace the more common two-story service structure at the back of the property.

Tropical sun drenches this little Caribbean gem, captured in an oil painting above the desk by New Orleans artist Michalopoulos (bottom). The unusual 1810 cottage departs from the typical form, having a long, rather than a square, layout. Missy Hodapp transformed the worn building into a modern home with accents of France and the timeless elegance of Seville.

Hodapp, with the help of architect Ed Wikoff and contractor David Trahan, created an interior without walls, where light flows above eight-foot cabinets and armoires. Glen Palmer built the cabinets based on the previous work of architect Frank W. Masson.

The dining room is reflected in a nineteenth-century pier mirror next to a window framing the crumbling brick and stucco of the house next door.

An open shower with a claw-footed tub adjoins Hodapp's bedroom. A grand Napoleon III cheval mirror with attached candelabras reflects the bed.

On this skinny lot (right), Hodapp's guest house is half the size of usual slave quarters. Glen Palmer built the staircase (top left) in the converted slave quarters. The bedroom in the slave quarters (bottom right) overlooks the courtyard. Cindy Lewis painted the headboard.

The Spanish Colonial House

An urban European derivative, the Spanish Colonial house joined the provincial-style cottage on the streets of the growing Vieux Carré, just after the great fire of 1794.

Around 1800 architect Barthelémy Lafon built this Spanish Colonial mansion (top left), now Waldhorn & Adler Antiques, for Vincent Rillieux, the great-grandfather of Edgar Degas. Rillieux also commissioned the building in the next block that is now Brennan's restaurant (top right). Dr. Joseph Montegut built this Spanish Colonial mansion (bottom left) on Royal Street in 1794. The Chesneau House (bottom right) on St. Louis Street is an example of sprawling Spanish Colonial architecture from 1800.

*An apartment in the Chesneau House is now the studio of photographer Josephine
Sacabo.*

Full of surprises, the Pedesclaux-LeMonnier House is the colossus of a transitional period. French architect Barthélémy Lafon designed the building, begun in 1794 and completed in 1811 by Latour and Laclotte. Called New Orleans' first skyscraper, this building shows strong Spanish Colonial influence with a new height attributed to both American style and advancing technology. The third floor's elliptical salon, with its domed ceiling, must have been a sensation in the nineteenth century. Never before seen in New Orleans, the dome was one of only ten in the United States at the time.

The fanciful third floor (left page) is the home of Jana Napoli, founder of a non-profit arts guild for inner city youth called YA/YA (Young Artists/Young Aspirations). YA/YA alumni helped Jana create this dreamscape. Brandon Thomas painted the sky ceiling and Rontherin Ratliff created canvas faux doors. Jana created the flower and animal dimensionals and a near life-size likeness as a memorial to her friend Lucita Cruz Monroy.

The oversized rooms of the French Quarter allow for audacious blending of styles and periods unified with color.

The third floor loggia of the Pedesclaux-LeMonnier house wraps around an interior courtyard.

The Townhouse

The Creole townhouse is a Spanish Colonial house with a plan. More compact and regularized, the townhouse evolved in the early nineteenth century. The early Creole townhouse makes the most of its space with two stories—commercial on the first floor and residential above. A walkway or carriageway leads to the courtyard, where an exterior stair leads to upper floors. A service wing along the side of the lot forms an L-shape. In many townhouses an entresol, or intermediate second floor lit by the tops of arched windows, accommodates storage.

Townhouses sprung up all over the French Quarter as New Orleans' population doubled several times in the first half of the nineteenth century. In the 1830s plantation owners splashed their wealth around town, constructing grand-scale townhouses for their visits to the big city. Americans added interior stairways and side halls. Still, like their traditions, Creole elements steadfastly remained.

The 1808 Nicholas House (top left). The back of an 1830 Decatur Street row house (top right) built by Gurlie and Guillot as rental property for the Ursuline nuns. This 1820 Toulouse Street house (bottom left) shows both a porte-cochère *and an* entresol. *This 1830 two-and-a-half-story townhouse (bottom right) on Dumaine Street blends Federal and Creole styles. Soniat House stair, 1829 (right).*

Painters and perfumes permeate the history of Peterson Moon Yokum's home. Yokum's mother, Rita Elizabeth Hovey-King, was a talented artist and the daughter of Mrs. Alvin Hovey-King of the Hové Parfumeurs. Yokum inherited his mother's creative gift for painting along with the Creole townhouse that has been in the family for generations.

Gunsmith Valery Nicholas built this commercial/residential building in 1808. The dining room was originally a bedroom and the kitchen off the dining room was a ladies' dressing room. The fan window lights an *azotea,* or upstairs porch, unique in the French Quarter.

Pictures of ancestors adorn the bedroom mantel. To the far right is an *odalisque* Yokum's mother painted for a speakeasy when she was a struggling young artist in New York.

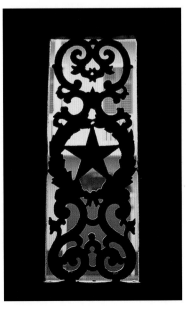

Original wrought iron ramshorn hinges and door latches add rugged detail to the interiors. The original gate in the *porte-cochère* was melted down for bullets during the Civil War.

In the Creole parlor, two of Yokum's works, a self-portrait and an image of his father created in the 1980s, lean against a French mirror, and over the mantel (right) is a portrait of Yokum's father painted forty years earlier by his mother.

A two hundred-year-old vampire might have just stepped out of this house to stroll on Jackson Square. Lucy Burnett's 1820s Creole townhouse is haunted by French-speaking ghosts and draped in antique lace. Palm fronds, kept after Palm Sunday, gather dust with relics and candles on an altar in the loggia.

The bedroom of Burnett's townhouse drips with eclectic Vieux Carré style. The painting above the mantel was commissioned by Napoleon's court and symbolizes the freedom of France.

Hanging on Burnett's bedroom wall is a tufted cushion with gilt brass flourishes used in nineteenth-century France to display a traditional bridal headpiece of delicate wax flowers and berries.

The courtyard of the Burnett
Townhouse.

The architecture and details of Gregory Holt's Creole townhouse remain much as Jean Chaigneau intended when he built the home in 1827 for Honore Landreaux, Jr. The back stair, an open loggia in Creole days, has been enclosed, and the upper porch is now Holt's office.

An eighteenth-century English refectory table and sideboard suit the scale of the expansive dining room. A Peterson Moon Yokum painting, *Walter Payton at Preservation Hall,* brings New Orleans jazz into the room opposite Empire-style drapes.

Owner Rodney Smith created rooms fit for Napoleon's court in the two Creole townhouses that comprise New Orleans' finest small hotel, the Soniat House. François Boisdoré, a free man of color, designed the main building for wealthy plantation owner Joseph Soniat Dufossat in 1829. The house across the street was built in 1834 for Dufossat's son.

Draper Alain Simard created the Empire campaign bed.

The Soniat House overlooks a subtropical courtyard from a cool, white porch, brightened by a French gesso console table and light-painted floors. Painted wood floors, for function and decoration, show up everywhere, from medieval Netherlands to early America. In late nineteenth-century Louisiana, painted wood was an alternative to austere natural wood, expensive marquetry, or carpeting. Painted floors have found a new vogue in today's understated elegance.

Virginie Avegno Gautreau, the subject of John Singer Sargent's scandalous masterpiece *Madame X,* was born in the four-story French Quarter townhouse now owned by antiques dealers Charles Robinson and Ron Julian. The home was built in 1825 for the Avegno family and today houses a stunning repository of modern creations, French antiques, and Oriental deco furnishings.

Aurora Leading the Chariot of Apollo, *a seventeenth-century copy of the Guido Reni ceiling in Rome, hangs in the dining room (top). Robinson designed the lighted glass table for his previous home, a Frank Lloyd Wright house, and boldly combines this modern statement with iron pillars from a Tulsa mansion and eighteenth-century balloon-back chairs (bottom). An Italian sconce of* Belle Époque *profusion spreads above a Chinese art deco commode. An early French art deco bench sits in the foreground (right).*

The balconies of "Gallery Row" evoke images of the hanging gardens of ancient Mesopotamia, dangling lush greenery over Royal Street. Jon Vaccari designed the interior of his 1831 townhouse with business partner Susanna Kost. The building's Creole character intimately blends luxurious fabrics, antiques, and contemporary art.

A royal lancer from a fanciful Indian regiment stands sentry at the second floor.

A Juan Laredo painting of green jesters celebrates New Orleans' Carnival in Vaccari's parlor.

The Vieux Carré combines the sophistication of a large city with the graciousness associated with subtropical climates. The unpretentious elegance and ages-old soul of the Quarter color the rhythms of daily life and allow each of its residents to discover his or her own uniqueness.
—*Jon Vaccari*

A David Halliday photograph flashes a contemporary gesture in an atmosphere of antiquity above a Louis XV writing table.

Contemporary art, Indonesian puppet dolls, and a family portrait decorate Vacarri's parlor, appointed with modern pieces and an 1860s French armoire.

Along the canals of Venice, second-story windows frame luxurious red walls ablaze with glittering chandeliers, stimulating fantasies of what wonderful things happen inside. The couple that bought this French Quarter home captured the mystery of Venice in vermilion . . . and wonderfulness ensued.

In 1834, Gabriel Correjolles, an architect from St. Dominique, designed this townhouse so that every room opens onto the exquisite courtyard. Sherwood Anderson entertained friends there during the bohemian renaissance of the Vieux Carré in the 1920s. Architect John E. Decell renovated the house in the 1970s.

An ancestral portrait hangs in the red room of the Casa Correjolles.

The red walls of the Casa Correjolles embrace the erotic jungle greens in a Grace Newberger painting. The palette of the walls and hall floors was realized by Darin Brunet.

129

New Orleans' premier architect/builder team Claude Gurlie and Joseph Guillot designed their *pièce de résistance* for Paul Prevost in 1834. This three-and-a-half story townhouse, with its marble mantels and delicate flourishes, invokes a time of lavish living and extravagant entertaining. Owner Nina Tyler worked with architect Leon Impastato and designer George Segers to escort these rooms into the twenty-first century with their European grace intact.

This spacious dining room reinvents Regency in contemporary French Quarter fashion. The streets are narrow in the Vieux Carré, making the balcony across Royal seem close enough to touch.

The interior stair and side hall of the Prevost house intimate an American-style townhouse, but the layout, carriageway, courtyard, and service wing all show Creole tradition still dominating.

After Tyler carefully scraped off the wallpaper from the third floor sitting room, generations of colors emerged to make the room an abstract portrait of history. Against this palette, contemporary Donghia furnishings frame the original slate mantel.

Designer Wilton Arnold never looks for a particular piece, nor does he try to fill a specific space. Rather, he adopts works that move him through their intrinsic joy, sadness, or even humor, and gives them a home in his apartment in the old servants' wing of the Prevost house. Arnold's parlor mixes Paulette Whiteman paintings and George Dureau drawings with antique Congolese artifacts. Norman Therrian made the organic side table, as well as the female sculpture (left). Beside the sculpture are three wood pieces by Matthew Vigi and a Mitch Gaudet image of the infant Beethoven.

The Olivier House has been called the most beautiful architecture in the Vieux Carré. Now a hotel, the Creole townhouse with a wide back stair was built in 1836. J.N.B dePouilly designed the home for Marianne Bienvenu, widow of Nicolas Godefroy Olivier, a rich plantation owner.

This four-story townhouse and the two homes next to it were built in 1838 for the family of Dr. Christian Miltenberger, who served as a surgeon at the Battle of New Orleans.

The Miltenberger House has the American-style side hall and interior stair.

Designed by owner Susan Hoffman and draper Alain Simard, the high French double parlor whispers romance with a blend of antiques and a gold-leaf ceiling.

A velvety bateau en lit *adds a Louis XV touch to the comfortable elegance of the Miltenberger House.*

A green mercury ball in the chandelier reflects the Belle Époque kitchen and its contemporary flair. The spheres were called "witches' balls" from an old belief that a witch would see a normal image of herself in the usually distorted reflection.

The attic of the Miltenberger House marries Moderne to traditional.

Robert Sonnier's eclectic assemblage of artifacts ranges from mother-of-pearl powder horns from the private guard of the Ottoman Empire to a Louis XV-style chandelier to a contemporary Robert Gordy painting. The space's earth-tone ambiance reflects Sonnier's personality and suffuses the graceful rooms of this 1842 side-hall townhouse built for Gabriel Montemart.

A Regency mirror hangs above the mantel. Directoire chairs face an Oriental-style coffee table. A shell of the largest nut in the world, called a *coco de mère,* serves as an abstract sculpture on the sideboard next to the ivory armlets of African royalty.

Looking like a setting for one of Scheherazade's Arabian tales, George and Marilyn Young's French Quarter parlor overflows with seductive opulence. *The Red Parrot* by Jules Laure, 1840, hangs in the Etruscan red parlor amidst new pieces and Third Empire antiques. The previous owners of the house, designer Hal Williamson and Dr. Dale LeBlanc, imported Scalamandre silk to create the ruched and fringed masterpieces—surely the French Quarter's most elaborate draperies.

The double parlor starts with seven shades of red trimmed in gold and moves to a 1710 Zuber design with a swirling scene of Bombay (pages 142-143). The second parlor's visual feast features Italian Bishop's chairs, seventeenth-century Venetian blackamoors, and a bar made from a coffin.

The Young's house was built in 1865 and replaced an 1840 cottage owned by a free woman of color, Françoise François, alias Manetta Laveau. The service building to that cottage still stands. The Youngs connected the out-building to the house with a rare second-story bridge passing over the courtyard.

Recent renovations of these two buildings by architect Frank W. Masson, of Barry Fox Associates, and builder Hackett Cummins won renovation and historic preservation awards.

The slave quarters has its original mantel and classic French Provincial decor.

Variations on the Theme: The Unconventional Townhouse

The Hermann-Grima House looks out of place in the Vieux Carré: it is set apart from its neighbors, having no common walls with other buildings, and has a Federal-style entrance that would be more at home in New England. Inside, however, the house shares a stylistic heritage with many Quarter structures—a typically American grand center hall and stairway once again mingle with the Creole-influenced back gallery and service structures.

German immigrant Samuel Hermann hired American architect William Brand to design his family home in 1831. Judge Felix Grima bought the house in 1840, and his family lived here for five generations.

Corinthian columns and ornate wood carving surround the sliding pocket doors of the double parlor. A bust of the Greek goddess Diana looks over the dining room reflected in a nine-teenth-century convex mirror.

The greater part of the book [Dinner at Antoine's] *has come into being in my study at Beauregard House in New Orleans—a study ideally located in the old slave quarters, at the rear of a pleasant patio dominated by an ancient fountain and surrounded with camellia bushes.*

—*Frances Parkinson Keyes,*
Foreword to Dinner at Antoine's, *1948*

The Beauregard-Keyes House is another handsome child from the mixed marriage of American and Creole sensibilities. Gabriel's brother, François Correjolles, also an architect, designed the home for Joseph Le Charpentier in 1826.

This bedroom boasts an American half-tester bed and faux marble baseboards.

Creole war hero General P. G. T. Beauregard rented rooms here for a short time after the war. A few decades later, novelist Frances Parkinson Keyes fell in love with the house and lived here in the 1940s and 1950s. Today, the house is a museum, appropriately bearing the names of both a Creole and an American.

The dining room was originally an open gallery overlooking the enclosed courtyard.

The late nineteenth-century boom in wealth and manufacturing technology spurred an American revival of practically every historic style. An Empire sofa and Jacobean-style dining chairs join Victorian pieces in the Beauregard-Keyes House, creating a nice chronicle of nineteenth-century American taste. At the same time, the rooms are arranged in the old Creole cottage style, with parlor and dining room on one side and bedrooms on the other.

One of New Orleans' most important architects, James Gallier, Jr., designed his own house in the French Quarter in 1857, a creative combination of the Creole and American townhouse in Greek Revival style.

Like any elegant lady spending time in the mud, heat, and humidity of a tropical colony, the Vieux Carré had to don summer dress. Rugs and carpets were covered with grass mats. Furniture was slip-covered in cool white cotton so expensive damasks and brocades were kept clean. And, with windows open for ventilation, paintings and chandeliers were draped with sheer gauze to protect them from insects.

Lion's mask molding crowns the period double parlor.

Hand-blocked wallpaper from 1855 turns the hallway between the Gallier House and service wing into Aramide's garden.

The necessity of the civilized swamp—mosquito netting—drapes a rare Rococo
Revival bed from the shop of Prudent Mallard, one of nineteenth-century
Louisiana's most significant furniture makers.

As the economy and population boomed, the townhouse found itself squeezed into tall Parisian-style apartments like the 1850 Pontalba and the 1840 LaBranche buildings. Behind St. Louis Cathedral, along Pirates' Alley, William Faulkner lived in an apartment in the LaBranche row, where he wrote his first novel, *Soldier's Pay*, and a series for the *Times-Picayune* called "New Orleans Sketches."

The Faulkner House winds playfully up four stories around a tiny courtyard, each floor with its own color and personality.

. . . all in her house is dim and beautiful with age. She reclines gracefully upon a dull brocade chaise-lounge, there is the scent of incense about her, and her draperies are arranged in formal folds. She lives in an atmosphere of a bygone and more gracious age.
—William Faulkner,
"New Orleans Sketches," 1925

The Faulkner House.

Gaelic mercury balls hang from the ceiling of the Louis XVI master bedroom resplendent in the stunning wash of hyacinth created by Rosemary James.

159

Overlooking the Cathedral garden, in bold Venetian colors, is one of the most fabulous rooms on earth. Rosemary James converted the corner apartment into her office and the show-room for Faulkner House Designs. Unvarnished wood floors are back in style. The beautifully raw, light-colored wood was left unfinished in the eighteenth and nineteenth centuries because the newly-cut boards took years to dry.

Wide, tree-lined Esplanade Avenue at the edge of the Vieux Carré became the desirable address for wealthy Creoles in grand antebellum New Orleans. In its prime, Esplanade topped St. Charles Avenue with its magnificent parade of Greek Revival, Italianate, and Victorian homes.

In 1879, architect William Fitzner designed this Esplanade Avenue townhouse for Charles Andrew Johnson, a Connecticut lawyer, who moved to New Orleans in 1840. Johnson died a bachelor in 1896, leaving his house to the woman he loved, Marie Landry Lanaux.

The current owner of the Lanaux Mansion, Ruth Bodenheimer, has a spiritual connection to the home. One evening, Bodenheimer saw a figure walking toward the attic. She recognized the clothing as that of a nineteenth-century gentleman. Years later, Bodenheimer met a Lanaux descendant who showed her a portrait of Johnson. She recognized the face as the ghost she had seen. Bodenheimer returned the painting to its original place in the parlor.

Charles Andrew Johnson's portrait, painted in 1885, returned to its original place. The photograph on the table was found in the attic and may be Marie Lanaux and one of her children.

The ghostly visit inspired Bodenheimer to restore Johnson's Esplanade Avenue townhouse to its Victorian prime. While decorating the house with designer Charles Kunz, she took cues from underlined passages in Johnson's books on design. Bodenheimer still finds treasures in the attic, where much of the original furniture was found. Every detail of the Lanaux mansion has been preserved, from the brass keys and servants' bell pulls, to the wallpaper, medallions, and marble mantels.

Camellias sit beside a Victorian lustre on the mosaic mantel in the dining room.

Service Structures

Every Creole house has its outbuildings or service wings, be they slave quarters, kitchens, stables, or *garçonnieres* (separate quarters for the young men of the household).

The service wing of the Gallier House (top left). The cottage at 801 Royal Street (top right) has a continuous wall at the street enclosing the courtyard between the cottage and its slave quarters. This cottage may be as old as 1788 and was at one time the furniture shop of Juan Bautista Durel. The Gallier House slave quarters (bottom left) are furnished as they would have been in the 1850s. A two-story service building at the Chateau Hotel (bottom right). The staircase of an 1824 garçonniere (right).

The Spanish Colonial service building behind Lucullus Antiques houses the shop's offices and a meeting room of pre-Raphaelite beauty. Seventeenth-century Spanish furnishings suit this rugged architecture. The original paint remains on the beam ceiling.

Patout's courtyard.

Antiques dealer Peter Patout lives in a frozen moment of Creole Louisiana history. Family portraits, antique toile, and plantation heirlooms fill his 1824 *garçonniere*.

In colonial Louisiana, natural grass rugs were favored over carpets to cover wood or marble floors. Barely above sea level, in the rainiest part of the United States, the unpaved streets of the French Quarter became flooded so often that the sidewalks are still called *banquettes*, like little river banks. Expensive imported carpets would not have fared well.

A Louisiana bautac chair, a relative of the Mexican campeche, sits opposite a Directoire couch. The Louisiana Federal lyre-back chairs were made for St. Louis Cathedral. Toile palmettes hang above the windows.

Eighteenth-century faïences *hang above the kitchen fireplace of Patout's* garçonniere. *Bay leaf and bittersweet dry on the mantel.*

A Mardi Gras mask hangs on a hurricane shade overlooking the bedroom. The mahogany bed came from Patout's hometown on Bayou Teche. A postmortem portrait of Patout's *tante* Charlotte Matilde Grevenberg (right) came from Albania Plantation.

William Faulkner, Lillian Hellman, F. Scott Fitzgerald, Gertrude Stein, and John Dos Passos found inspiration in New Orleans in the 1920s. Later, Tennessee Williams, Truman Capote, John Kennedy Toole, and Walker Percy danced with the French Quarter muse.

Vogue writer Julia Reed, one of the French Quarter's current generation of literati, lives in a slave quarter apartment that was once the home of Sherwood Anderson.

A jungle of fruit trees and flowers surround the vibrant red and green building (its original 1830 colors) in stark contrast to the white, island elegance of the interior.

In 1963, Yale architect John E. Decell added the graceful interior stair to Reed's apartment when he renovated this building for his family, who still own the property. Decell's renovation maintained the integrity of the old building that has one of the French Quarter's only remaining pan-tile roofs.

Reed's comfortable office/library (above). The mantel (left) serves as an altar. The dining room (top, facing page) is simply decorated with engravings. The carriageway (bottom, facing page) cuts through the middle of the first floor.

The circa-1800 Toussaint Mossy building sits far behind shops on Royal Street. This carriage-house and slave quarters looked like a blank canvas to art dealer Barbara Louviere. Her collection of bright, rebellious works by self-taught Louisiana artists filled that tabula rasa with emotion when Louviere moved in. Above the mantel is a painting by Reginald Gee. The fish were carved by Ivy Billot.

The metal dogs and angelfish are the work of Stephanie Constanzi. The Archer (upper right) was created by David Butler.

Ersy Schwartz's The Asylum.

The Fisk-Hopkins house, circa 1860, served as a *garçonnière* and billiard room for the men of the Alvarez Fisk family, who lived in the mansion next door.

The parlor charms with its antebellum grace and magnificent plaster molding. A second floor was added in the 1870s. The home has been in the Schwartz family since 1925. A long baroque garden in front makes the house a unique sight in the French Quarter. Throughout the house, Eugénie Schwartz's antiques contrast with the contemporary art of her daughter, Ersy Schwartz.

The mahogany dining room table on wagon wheel legs was built by a family friend,
the celebrated artist Enrique Alferez, and rivals the beautily-carved Teutonic china
cabinet and sideboard.

Shotgun

Georges told Marie Louise that the houses were named that way because, from the front, the single ones made you think of single-barreled shotguns and the double ones of double-barreled shotguns; but Omer said this was all nonsense, that they were called 'shotgun' houses because the rooms in them were placed one straight behind another, and therefore, a shot fired in the front room could—and often did!—hit a man in the back room. Marie Louise liked the second explanation much better than she did the first one, and as she went by the row of 'shotgun' houses she listened, half hopefully and half fearfully, for a shot to ring out.

—Frances Parkinson Keyes, Once on Esplanade, 1947

In the post-Civil War depression the shotgun house became popular all over New Orleans. Its long, skinny shape, probably from the West Indies, squeezed perfectly into the ever-narrowing lots of the French Quarter.

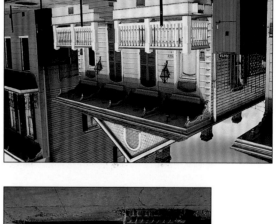

Shotgun single (top left). An 1890s shotgun double (top right). Shotgun double, 1890 (bottom left). A shotgun with a Classical Revival flourish built around 1910 (bottom right). The back door of a typical shotgun (right).

THE MUSIC IN MOTION

As an historic storehouse the Vieux Carré represents a cumulative effect, not an isolated moment of history, but a kind of mobile moment, ever receding into the background, or moving forward, depending on how one prefers to see it. Here we find a colorful kaleidoscopic blending, not only of many periods, styles and historic associations, but also the varied types and activities of huckster and barbers, artists and shopkeepers, shopgirls, antique dealers, tourists, evening crowds. This very diversity is not only a true image of what we have been; it is also a keynote to the distinctive flavor and picturesque appeal that have been sensed by so many observers. . . . we don't want another Williamsburg—a museum village, perfectly "preserved," in all of its details. The problem is—how do you preserve a kaleidoscope? Obviously, to keep it, you must keep it in motion.

—Bernard Lemann, Professor Emeritus, Tulane School of Architecture
The Vieux Carré—A General Statement, 1966

The Vieux Carré changes and shifts, every day revealing some new magic in the movement of the old. There is no end to the colors and tones of the French Quarter rhapsody. And the music plays on and on. ❧

A window on Royal Street from the Prevost House.

Our Lady of Victory Church at the Ursuline Convent.

BIBLIOGRAPHY

Arthur, Stanley Clisby. *Old New Orleans, Walking Tours of the French Quarter.* Fourteenth printing. Gretna: Pelican Publishing Company, 1995 (c. 1936).

Chase, John Churchill. *Frenchmen, Desire, Good Children and Other Streets of New Orleans.* New York: Macmillan, third edition, 1979.

Heard, Malcom. *French Quarter Manual.* New Orleans: Tulane School of Architecture, 1997.

Huber, Leonard V. *New Orleans, a Pictorial History.* Gretna: Pelican Publishing Company, 1991 (c. 1971).

Kennedy, Richard S. Ed. *Literary New Orleans: Essays and Meditations.* Baton Rouge: Louisiana State University Press, 1992.

——————— *Landmarks of New Orleans.* New Orleans: Louisiana Landmark Society, 1984.

Lemann, Bernard. *The Vieux Carré—A General Statement.* New Orleans: Tulane University, 1966.

New Orleans City Guide, Written and Compiled by the Federal Writers' Project of the Works Progress Administration for the City of New Orleans. Boston: Houghton Mifflin Company, 1952.

Ricciuti, Italo William. *New Orleans and Its Environs, The Domestic Architecture 1727-1870.* New York: Bonanza Books, 1967.

Saxon, Lyle. *Lafitte the Pirate.* Gretna: Pelican Publishing Company, 1994 (c. 1930).

Siegel, Martin. *New Orleans: A Chronological & Documentary History 1539-1970.* New York: Oceana Publications, 1975.

Stevens, Patricia Land. *Louisiana's Architectural and Archaeological Legacies.* Northwestern State University Press, 1982.

Tallant, Robert. *Mardi Gras.* Gretna: Pelican Publishing Company, 1976.

Toledano, Roulhac. *The National Trust Guide to New Orleans.* New York: John Wiley & Sons, 1996.

The WPA Guide to New Orleans, The Federal Writers' Project Guide to 1930s New Orleans. New York: Pantheon Books.

Vogt, Lloyd. *New Orleans Houses, A House-Watcher's Guide.* Gretna: Pelican Publishing Company, 1985.

Like icicles in a tropical courtyard, contradic-
tions intensify New Orleans' beauty—the sacred
and the profane, the modern and the ancient.

The Majesty of the
FRENCH
QUARTER